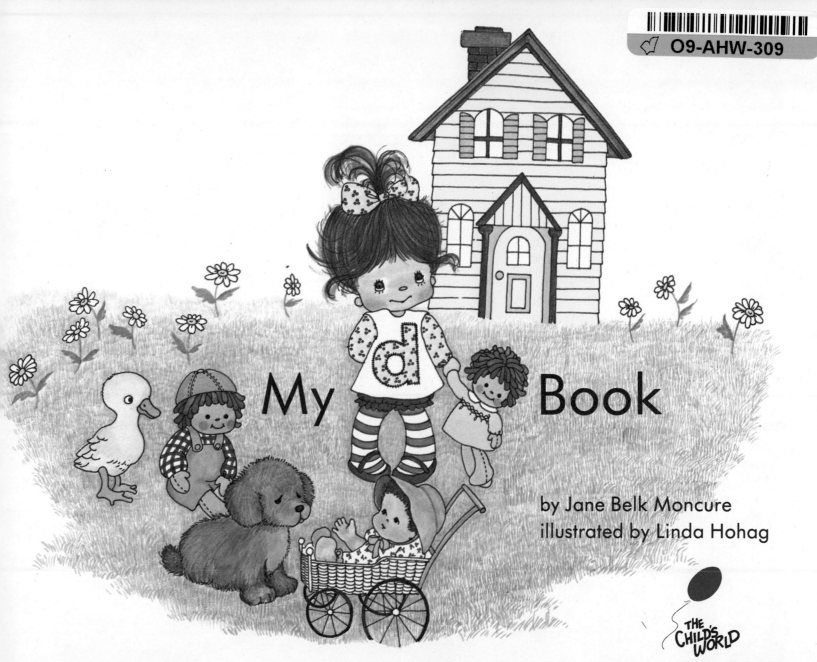

My d Book

by Jane Belk Moncure

illustrated by Linda Hohag

THE CHILD'S WORLD

ELGIN, ILLINOIS 60120

Library of Congress Cataloging in Publication Data

Moncure, Jane Belk.
  My "d" book.

  (My first steps to reading)
  Rev. ed. of: My d sound box. © 1978.
  Summary: Little d plays with many things beginning
with the letter d.
  1. Children's stories, American.   [1. Alphabet]
I. Hohag, Linda. ill.   II. Moncure, Jane Belk.   My d
sound box.   III. Title.   IV. Series: Moncure, Jane
Belk.   My first steps to reading.
PZ7.M739Myd   1984   [E]   84-17544
ISBN 0-89565-279-X

Distributed by Childrens Press, 1224 West Van Buren Street,
Chicago, Illinois 60607.

My "d" Book

(Blends are included in this book.)

Little  had a box'

It was a big box.

She said, "I will fill my  box."

Little found dolls...

lots of dolls,

dolls, dolls.

One doll danced.

One doll played a drum.

Little  put the dolls into her box.

But some dolls
fell out.

Little said, "This box
is too little.

"I will make
a big
doll house
for my
dolls."

Little  made a doll desk

and dresser.

14

She made a table and  some

dishes for the dolls.

Little made doll dresses ...

lots of doll dresses.

Then she dressed her dolls

and took them for a drive.

Little 👧 made toys for her dolls.

She made

ducks

and dogs for
her dolls.

The dolls played with the dogs.

One doll got sick.

She took the
doll to a doctor.

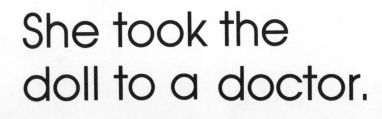

One doll had a toothache.

Little doll took the doll to a dentist.

One day Little opened the door. She found a dollar and a dime.

"I will buy  donuts," she said.

And she did!

dolls

dog

Now she had donuts

doll
dresses

desk

ducks

dresser

for all her dolls.

More words with Little

diamond

domino

deer

diary

daisy

dustpan

dove

dwarf

donkey

dandelion

doghouse

dinosaur

29